Small   Tender   Goodly   Nicely

THE GIFT OF WINTER

by
John Leach and Jean Rankin

Prentice-Hall, Inc., Englewood Cliffs, New Jersey

10   9   8   7   6   5   4   3   2   1   83   82   81   80   79   78   77

Library of Congress Cataloging in Publication Data

Leach, John.
  The gift of winter.

  SUMMARY: Two children join an expedition to lodge a
formal complaint against winter.
  [1. Winter — Fiction. 2. Snow — Fiction.]
I. Rankin, Jean, joint author. II. Title.
PZ7.L4612Gi3   [E]   77-6266

  ISBN 0-13-354886-4

There was once a time when winter was cold, bleak, and desolate. Everybody hated winter, especially Small and Tender. They couldn't have any fun playing outdoors.

When the people of their town decided to complain to Winter personally, Small and Tender secretly made their plans to go too.

Tromp, tromp, tromp, tromp, tromp, tromp, tromp,

tromp, tromp, tromp, tromp, tromp, tromp, tromp.

Small and Tender made peanut butter sandwiches, collected their tent and warm socks and followed the others. No one knew they had left town. They walked and walked and walked.

Steppidy steppidy step, steppidy steppidy step.

Small and Tender could not walk as fast as the others. They began to get very tired. "I can't see them anywhere," said Small.

"Let's take a short cut through the woods and catch up," said Tender. Soon they were in the middle of a large forest. It was very dark in there.

"I'm scared," said Tender, and began to cry.

"I think we are lost," said Small. "HELP! HELP!"

"Who's making all that noise down there?" growled a voice above their heads. "We're trying to sleep."

"We're lost," sniffled Tender.

"Who are you?" quavered Small.

"I'm Maple," said the voice. "Spruce and I will help you. Hey, wake up, Spruce." When all the trees had woken up, the children explained that they were on a protest march to the Ministry of Winter. "It's late," said Maple. "You'd better camp here for the night under the safety of our branches, and we'll help you on your way in the morning."

"Oh, you're a sugar, Maple!" sighed Spruce.

The children slept comfy in their tent and the wind blew high over head. The next morning they walked through the forest, guided by the friendly trees.

"Merry Christmas, trees," they shouted at the edge of the forest. "Goodbye, thank you, Merry Christmas."

The children marched on over the bleak and rocky countryside, until in the distance they saw the others sitting around a campfire.

When they came close, everyone cried out:
"SMALL AND TENDER! HOW DID YOU GET HERE?"

"This is all we need!" raged Malicious.

"Go on home," snarled Rotten.

"Oh, but they've come so far," sighed Nicely.

Bazooey spoke up. "Fret not, my little ones. You stick with me and I'll take care of you."

"Oh, it's all my fault," said Goodly. "We'll never be home by Christmas."

"You mustn't blame yourself, Goodly," Nicely assured him. "I know we'll make it."

Suddenly Bazooey yelled in excitement.
He pointed off into the distance.

When the heavy front doors of the Ministry clanged shut they found themselves in an enormous hall. "You don't have an appointment?" questioned an icy voice. "Well, then, you'll have to fill out the forms for the Secretary of Cold."

Then the voice, sounding slightly more amiable, began to sing:
"Go straight down the tunnel
and turn to the right,
on down the hall
and up one flight;
keep on going past the file department door
and take the elevator to the fifteenth floor;
go right, then left, then straight down the hall,
you'll see the Secretary's sign hanging on the wall."

They thought they'd never get there. But at last they came to the right door, for on the wall they saw a sign which read: THE SECRETARY OF COLD.

Nervously they filed through the door. The Secretary of Cold was very annoyed at being interrupted. "See Winter? Impossible!" she shrieked. "It's Christmas and I'm busy putting out a cold front."

"We came to fill out forms," Goodly began.

"Forms? Forms? Why didn't you say so." The Secretary beamed. Producing a bundle of papers, she sang:

"Here's one for you and two for me
and six for you and some for me.
Fill in every space you see
from one to a hundred and ninety-three."

They answered all the questions, filled in all the spaces and handed the forms to the Secretary, who took them away to be processed.

Nothing was happening. Impatiently Bazooey examined the controls and equipment around the room.

"Bazooey! You're not supposed to touch stuff that isn't yours," warned Tender.

"Can I see?" begged Small.

Bazooey pressed a big red button.

"WHAT DO YOU WANT?" boomed a deep voice that came from nowhere.

"Uh, uh, there are some people here with a complaint," Bazooey stammered, trying to sound like the Secretary.

"A complaint! A complaint? Send them in immediately!" The big doors to Winter's room slid open. Only Goodly, Nicely, Rotten, and Malicious went through them. The doors slammed shut.

Goodly and Nicely, hand in hand, stood in front of the huge throne. Winter towered above them.

"What's this I hear about a complaint?" he growled.

It was Nicely who first found her voice. "We have come to protest the dreary, bleak, and desolate conditions of winter. We request that proper and effective methods be initiated to make winter nicer."

There was a long silence.

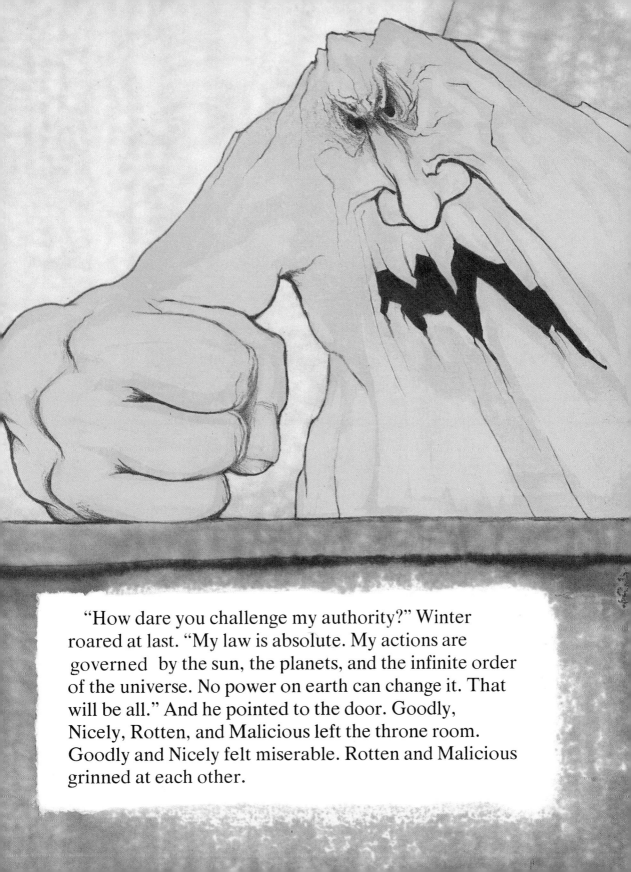

"How dare you challenge my authority?" Winter roared at last. "My law is absolute. My actions are governed by the sun, the planets, and the infinite order of the universe. No power on earth can change it. That will be all." And he pointed to the door. Goodly, Nicely, Rotten, and Malicious left the throne room. Goodly and Nicely felt miserable. Rotten and Malicious grinned at each other.

Left behind by the others, Bazooey, Small, and Tender entered another door. They were in the throne room, although they did not know it. "This place gives me the creeps," whispered Small.

"It's the dreariest, coldest place in the world," agreed Tender.

"It's just plain awful," stated Bazooey.

Small shivered. "Winter must be really mean, to make everything so awful." Above their heads Winter heard voices and began to listen.

"Well, maybe he can't help it," said Bazooey. "Maybe he's unhappy and lonely. That kind of thing hurts and sometimes makes people mean."

"Don't you think he has any friends?" asked Small.

"Nobody likes Winter," declared Tender.

"We'd all be unhappy if nobody liked us," said Bazooey. "How would you feel if nobody liked you?"

Winter's face grew longer and longer. A tear rolled down his cheek.

As it dropped, Winter's tear burst into tiny white stars. More tears fell from his eyes, and each one became a shower of sparkling white soft twinkly bits that slowly drifted through the air and came to rest all around. On Bazooey's head. On Tender's nose. On Small's little hands. "What's this stuff?" asked Bazooey.

At that moment the door opened and the Secretary of Cold entered, followed by Goodly, Nicely, Rotten, and Malicious. "Winter, are you all right?" the Secretary asked. "What is this stuff, do you know?" she added.

Winter raised his head and the stars stopped falling.

"No," he whispered.

"What did he say?" asked Goodly.

"The answer is no," the Secretary announced.

"The answer is s'no?" Bazooey asked.

"The answer is snow?" Small wanted to know. Then:

"THE ANSWER IS SNOW." they all shouted together.

Winter smiled and a little more snow appeared like magic. Winter began to chuckle, and snow filled the air. Winter roared with laughter and the room became a beautiful whirling blizzard.

"Let's take some home to Mommy and Daddy for Christmas," said Tender.

"Oh, Tender, today is Christmas," said Nicely. "We'll never get home in time."

"I'll get you home," boomed Winter happily. "I feel wonderful," and he led them all outside.

As they whirled and slid and flew towards home,
Winter shouted at the top of his voice:
"It's good to laugh,
it's good to cry,
it makes me feel so free;
it's ever so good,
it's ever so good,
it's ever so good to be me."

At home their neighbors greeted them and cheered the freshly fallen snow. "Thank you, Winter," they all shouted. Waving good bye, Winter turned homeward.

Ever after, when winter came, the snow came too. Snow made winter beautiful. People invented skis and toboggans. They threw snowballs and made snowmen. Children had fun outdoors. Winter echoed with happy laughter.